U.S. Fish & Wildlife Service

Writing Refuge Management Goals and Objectives:

A Handbook

The mission of the National Wildlife Refuge System
is to administer a national network of lands and
waters for the conservation, management, and
where appropriate, restoration of the fish, wildlife,
and plant resources and their habitats within the
United States for the benefit of present and future
generations of Americans.

National Wildlife Refuge System Improvement Act of 1997
(Public Law 105-57, October 9, 1997)

Table of Contents

Authors

U.S. Fish and Wildlife Service
Robert S. Adamcik
Elizabeth S. Bellantoni
Don C. DeLong Jr.
John H. Schomaker

U.S. Geological Survey
David B. Hamilton
Murray K. Laubhan
Richard L. Schroeder

Introduction

Goals and objectives are the unifying elements of successful refuge management. They identify and focus management priorities, provide a context for resolving issues, guide specific projects, provide rationale for decisions, and offer a defensible link among management actions, refuge purpose(s), Service policy, and the National Wildlife Refuge System (Refuge System) mission. Pursuant to Refuge Planning Policy (602 FW 1, 3, 4), this handbook offers guidance on how to write goals and objectives for national wildlife refuges and provides counsel on their development. While the handbook specifically addresses biology and visitor services, you can also utilize this guidance when developing goals and objectives for other refuge programs.

Several assumptions are basic to this handbook. The handbook focuses on the mechanics of writing sound goals and objectives. Detailed guidance on what information to consider, collect, interpret, and synthesize into goals and objectives is beyond the scope of this handbook. It views a vision statement as the synthesis of a refuge's purpose(s), the Refuge System mission and goals, and other biological, legal, and social concerns in which the refuge has a role. It also assumes a familiarity with the hierarchical nature of planning and where, within a planning process, the writing of goals and objectives occurs.

This guidance applies to conceptual management plans, comprehensive conservation plans (CCPs), step-down management plans (e.g., habitat management, visitor services, fire management), or any other planning document incorporating goals and objectives, including strategic documents developed under the Government Performance and Results Act. We intend this guidance for use by an internal audience tasked with writing refuge goals and objectives, primarily refuge managers, biologists, visitor services specialists, planners, and other members of refuge planning teams. Still, it recognizes that we should write goals and objectives so that interested members of the public can understand them, to the extent this does not jeopardize the technical accuracy or reduce the inclusion of necessary information. The terminology and definitions used in this handbook are widely accepted in the planning field and are not inconsistent with more recent application in strategic planning. Perhaps most important, the handbook presumes all goals and objectives must further the specific purpose(s) of the refuge and the broader mission of the Refuge System, as well as be consistent with Refuge Planning Policy and any other relevant Service policy and directives.

Section I

Goals and Objectives Within the Planning Process

Fish and Wildlife Service Mission
▼
Refuge System Mission
▼
Refuge Purpose(s)*
▼
National/Regional Goals and Priorities
▲▼
Ecosystem Goals and Objectives
▼
Refuge Vision
▼
Goals
▼
Objectives
▼
Strategies
▼
Monitoring and Feedback
(Adaptive Management)

Figure 1. Hierarchical relationship of refuge goals and objectives to other aspects of the planning process. (*When in conflict, refuge purpose(s) supercedes Refuge System mission.)

Management decisions should bring a refuge closer to its vision. Well-developed goals and objectives play a key role in accomplishing this by guiding management actions to help a refuge achieve its vision and ultimately, the purpose(s) for which it was established.

In developing goals and objectives, there is a natural progression from the general to the specific (Figure 1). First, we develop a vision that broadly reflects the refuge purpose(s), the Refuge System mission and goals, other statutory requirements, and larger-scale plans, as appropriate. Our goals then define general targets in support of the vision, followed by objectives that direct effort into incremental and measurable steps toward achieving those goals. Finally, strategies identify specific tools or actions to accomplish objectives.

In practice, the relationship among vision, goals, and objectives is iterative and dynamic. During the planning process you may revisit each as a plan develops or as new information becomes available. However, it is critical that you initiate the process at the beginning and preserve the hierarchical nature of the relationship demonstrated in Figure 1. It is important not to choose strategies without objectives, develop objectives without goals, or establish goals without first articulating a vision. Otherwise, two common errors may result: (1) You may develop goals to justify existing management programs and then create a vision that incorporates them; and/or (2) You may choose strategies you already are using (e.g., burning, grazing, partnerships), and then develop objectives to justify them. The result may be a plan that validates existing management practices, instead of one that objectively considers alternative actions and then directs effort toward achieving refuge purpose(s) and vision. Articulating a vision based upon refuge purpose(s) and other mandates will allow you to identify existing programs that may need to be refocused or eliminated.

Sound goal and objective development requires extensive review of preplanning data. Address the range of information gathered during the preplanning phase and continue to gather more, if necessary. Review the refuge purpose(s) and the Refuge System mission and goals, as well as statutes, regulations and policies that constrain or direct refuge management. Then examine the biological elements underlying refuge activities, larger-scale plans, and Regional priorities. Identify opportunities to facilitate compatible, priority public uses. Finally, review issues identified throughout the scoping process so you can be certain your goals and objectives adequately address them. Through such thoughtful examination, one can establish priorities and develop goals and objectives accordingly.

Goals and objectives are the heart of any plan, and their development takes critical thinking and analysis. A thoughtful effort will produce a defensible plan whose goals and objectives are clearly linked to the refuge vision and attainment of refuge purpose(s). Well-written goals and objectives can provide long-term guidance to refuge managers and staff and help integrate science, improve management practices, and justify compatible use decisions.

Section II
Terminology

Developing defensible goals and objectives requires an understanding of the relationships among several key terms. We excerpt the following definitions from the Refuge Planning Overview, 602 FW 1.6:

Alternatives. Different sets of objectives and strategies or means of achieving refuge purposes and goals, helping fulfill the Refuge System mission, and resolving issues.

Goal. Descriptive, open-ended, and often broad statement of desired future conditions that conveys a purpose, but does not define measurable units.

Objective. A concise statement of what we want to achieve, how much we want to achieve, when and where we want to achieve it, and who is responsible for the work. Objectives derive from goals and provide the basis for determining strategies, monitoring refuge accomplishments, and evaluating the success of strategies.

Refuge Purpose(s). The purposes specified in or derived from the law, proclamation, executive order, agreement, public land order, donation document, or administrative memorandum establishing, authorizing, or expanding a refuge, refuge unit, or refuge subunit.

Strategy. A specific action, tool, technique, or combination of actions, tools, and techniques used to meet unit objectives.

Vision Statement. A concise statement of what the planning unit should be, or what we hope to do, based primarily upon the Refuge System mission and specific refuge purposes, and other mandates.

Section III
Goals

Goals describe the desired future conditions of a refuge in succinct statements. Each one translates to one or more objectives that define these conditions in measurable terms. A well-written goal directs work toward achieving the vision and purpose(s) of a refuge and/or the System mission. Collectively, a set of goals is a framework within which to make decisions.

It takes careful thought to develop goals, yet it is a critical step. In a few concise statements, goals comprise the whole of a refuge's effort in pursuit of its vision and lay the foundation from which all refuge activities arise. Resource management, educational, recreational, maintenance, and administrative activities result *from* goals, and not the other way around. You must develop goals before developing objectives and strategies, so you can assess management direction against them, both during plan development and throughout implementation. Avoid rationalizing current or desired management activities and then creating goals (and objectives) to support them.

Purpose and Nature of Goals

By providing a framework within which we develop objectives, goals focus thinking about management actions and help promote defensible decisions. An individual goal supports the refuge vision and describes the desired end result. A goal may reference one or more habitats, wildlife groups, or elements of a visitor services program; an off-refuge land protection initiative; a wilderness program; or other conservation emphasis stemming from legal directives. While goals are broad statements, they must clearly and concisely define the ultimate targets of refuge management. They also should be broad enough to encompass a range of alternative sets of objectives and strategies for accomplishing the refuge purpose(s) and contributing to the Refuge System mission and goals.

A goal not only identifies a target, but also suggests a general direction of work. This avoids ambiguity and uncertainty. A refuge with Eastern deciduous hardwood forest as a core habitat component and a vision that states that it will contribute to the needs of hardwood-dependent Neotropical migratory birds might have a visitor services goal, *"To provide high-quality education and interpretive programs to visitors."* However, this goal is weak because it is too general. It could apply anywhere in the Refuge System, and it gives no direction to the content of visitor services programs that might be unique to this particular refuge. A better goal might be, *"Visitors understand and appreciate the importance of Eastern deciduous hardwood forests to songbirds and the refuge's role in conserving hardwood habitats."* This goal gives direction to the content of the education and interpretive programs and generally specifies our target. The goal does not specify the means to achieve the desired outcome; therefore, it does not limit consideration of alternative ways of working toward that outcome. If, for example, the goal were inappropriately written as, *"Through interpretive displays, visitors gain an understanding of and appreciation for. . .,"* we would not consider a range of additional strategies.

Appropriate Number of Goals

Refuge planning policy (602 FW 3) states that each refuge, at minimum, should develop goals, as appropriate, for:

- Wildlife species or groups of species
- Habitat (including land protection needs)
- Compatible wildlife-dependent recreation

Goals:

- Direct work toward achieving the vision and purpose(s) of a refuge and/or System mission

- State desired future conditions (what the refuge should be like)

- Are descriptive, open-ended, and often broad statements

- Convey a purpose, but do not define measurable units

- Are clear and understandable to the public

- Other mandates (e.g., refuge-specific legislation, executive orders, cultural resources, and special area designations such as wilderness)

- Fish, wildlife, and plant populations

We may combine two or more of these into a single goal, or we may write more than one goal for any of these. Policy does not suggest a minimum or maximum number. Rather, the number of goals required will be those necessary to address the above categories and achieve the refuge's vision, thus meeting its purpose(s) and the Refuge System mission.

Elements of Goals

Biological Goals

Habitat and wildlife management are closely intertwined. Managing wildlife may include habitat manipulation and direct manipulation of populations. Thus, where possible, biological goals should include *both* habitat and wildlife elements. For example, consider the goal, *"Restore refuge prairie to historic conditions to support pre-European settlement abundance and diversity of grassland-dependent migratory birds."* This goal contains both a habitat (prairie) and a wildlife (migratory birds) element.

At times we may wish to manage a landscape or community for its intrinsic ecological value and only implicitly for the wildlife it supports. In such cases, the goal might reference wildlife more generally, as in *"Protect and restore the remaining rare and fragile vernal pool communities of the central San Joaquin Valley and their associated wildlife complex."* In other instances, a goal may emphasize a wildlife target and leave identification of the habitat to objectives (e.g., *"Provide optimal feeding habitat for winter dabbling and diving ducks as the refuge's contribution to maximizing overwinter survival of these species in the Central Valley."*) Use sound professional judgment and the guidelines presented in this handbook to choose an appropriate approach.

Table 1. Examples of Key Elements of Biological Goals.

Subject	*Attribute*	*Target*	*Action*
Wildlife species or	Species diversity	Natural	Restore
group	Species richness	Historic range of variability	Maintain
-individual species	Population levels	Existing	Perpetuate
-taxonomic group	Productivity	Maximum	Provide
-guild	Population status	Period of time (e.g., 1970s)	Contribute
-community	Diversity/Composition	Viable	Aid
	Structure	Optimum (for a given species/group)	Achieve
Habitat or Ecosystem	Integrity	High quality (for a given species/group)	
-grassland	Health	Proper (e.g., proper functioning)	
-riparian	Functioning of processes		
-wetland			

Table 1 serves as a guide for developing and assessing biological goals. Each biological goal should contain four elements: (1) a key *subject* of concern (e.g., a particular species or guild, a biotic community, or a habitat type); (2) the *attribute* of interest for that subject (e.g., population size, physical area covered, species composition); (3) a conceptual *target* or condition for the attribute (e.g., a number, period of time, natural); and (4) an *action* or effort (e.g., restore, provide) that we will make relative to the target.

Below are two examples of biological goals that include all the key elements.

Biological Goals Rewritten to Contain All the Key Elements

<u>Example 1.</u>

Existing Goal: *Protection and maintenance of the bottomland forest avifauna.*

Goal Rewritten, Incorporating the Key Elements: *Maintain the existing level of species richness of migratory birds in refuge bottomland hardwood forest.*

<u>Example 2.</u>

Existing Goal: *The habitat management goal is to provide the life requirements of native migratory birds.*

Goal Rewritten, Incorporating the Key Elements: *Contribute to the restoration of natural species diversity of migratory birds in managed wetland habitats of the Basin and Range Physiographic Area.*

Visitor Services Goals

A visitor services goal should identify our intended audience and make clear what we want the audience to do, know, or feel. We can assess visitor services goals against the key elements listed in Table 2. Each goal will contain three elements: (1) an *audience* (e.g., visitors, local community); (2) an audience *reaction* (e.g., knows, understands,

Table 2. Examples of Key Elements of Visitor Services Goals.

Audience	*Reaction*	*Object of Reaction*
Visitors	Know	Basic ecological concepts
Wildlife-dependent recreationists	Understand	Fish and wildlife
Residents of the local community	Appreciate	The refuge
People living within 25 miles of the refuge	Enjoy	The Refuge System
Landowners in the watershed	Value	Best management practices
Students	Apply	Ethical outdoor behavior
	Display	Wildlife-dependent recreation
	Support	Refuge management
	Respond	
	Initiate	
	Seek	
	Demonstrate	

enjoys); and (3) an *object* of the reaction (e.g., ecological concepts, ethical behavior, wildlife-dependent recreation).

Visitor services goals also should focus on the expected outcome, not on the process that leads to the outcome (i.e., what visitors experience or learn as a result of an activity such as recreation, rather than on the activity). Next are two examples of visitor services goals that we have rewritten to focus more on the desired outcome rather than on the process or means by which we achieve the outcome. The process by which the desired outcome is achieved is appropriately developed as a strategy or strategies. The rewritten examples also clarify the intended audience by including the key elements of visitor services goals from Table 2.

Visitor Services Goals Rewritten to Focus on the Desired Outcome and that Contain All the Key Elements:

Example 1.

Existing Goal: *Provide educational opportunities for refuge visitors to learn about and enjoy the tallgrass prairie wetland ecosystem, the fish and wildlife found there, and the history of the refuge.*

Goal Rewritten, Focusing on the Desired Outcome: *Visitors of all abilities enjoy their refuge visit and increase their knowledge about the tallgrass prairie ecosystem and the refuge's history.*

Example 2.

Existing Goal: *To encourage an appreciation of the refuge, its fish and wildlife resources, and its management activities through quality recreational and educational programs.*

Goal Rewritten, Focusing on the Desired Outcome and Providing Clarity about the Intended Audience: *Visitors, students, and nearby residents value the refuge and its prairie conservation efforts.*

Section IV

Objectives

Objectives are incremental steps we take to achieve a goal. They derive from goals and provide a foundation for determining strategies, monitoring refuge accomplishments, and evaluating success. The number of objectives per goal will vary, but should be those necessary to achieve the goal. Where there are many, an implementation schedule might prove useful.

Objectives written using this guidance will have many applications. When developing objectives for a CCP, we generally write objectives that can be accomplished during the life of the plan. There will be exceptions, however, as when writing objectives for restoring habitats, which may require decades to reach the desired composition and function. In such cases, you may wish to specify a 15-year time frame for the application of selected strategies, or perhaps describe conditions desired at the end of 15 years that would suggest whether or not the course of action you have chosen is appropriate.

Properties that All Objectives Must Possess

All objectives must possess five properties. Each objective must be:

(1) Specific
(2) Measurable
(3) Achievable
(4) Results-oriented
(5) Time-fixed

These properties constitute the acronym "SMART," and we describe them below. We provide examples of biological and visitor services objectives and how well they meet the SMART criteria in Appendices A and B.

Specific. Avoid ambiguity by wording objectives clearly. A clearly worded objective is easy to understand and the meaning is difficult to misinterpret. Specificity results by including WHO will do the action, WHAT we will do, WHEN and WHERE we will do it, and WHY we will do it. (WHO may implicitly be the refuge staff, and "WHEN" we might integrate into an implementation schedule or the description of a strategy.) Avoid or minimize general phrases like "maintain high-quality habitat," "for the benefit of migratory birds," or "improve the visitor experience," as these phrases are subject to interpretation.

Measurable. Objectives should contain a measurable element that we can readily monitor to determine success or failure. Otherwise, you cannot tell if the strategies employed are appropriate, when we have met an objective, or if we should modify it. In evaluating measurability, ask, "What would we monitor to assess progress toward achieving this objective?" For example, you could not determine progress toward "high-quality habitat" or a "high-quality" visitor experience unless you have measurable criteria for "high quality." The nature of the measurable element may vary, as might the difficulty in measuring it. Still, you must have something to indicate progress. While evaluating a water depth objective may only require gauge readings, monitoring a component of vegetative structure may require systematic surveys of vegetation density or composition.

Achievable. Objectives, no matter how measurable or clearly written, must be achievable. If you cannot resolve constraints on achieving an objective, then you must discard or rewrite it. Do not ask more of the land or wildlife than it can deliver, and use sound professional judgment to develop reasonable expectations

of time, staff, and funds available to pursue the objective. However, some *apparent* constraints may be surmountable. Consider an objective to reduce refuge contaminants originating off-refuge. Though outside Service authority, this objective may be achievable through partnerships with other Federal agencies, the State, or private stakeholders.

Results-oriented. Objectives should specify an end result. For example, a habitat objective that is results-oriented will provide a detailed description of the desired habitat conditions expected. When reading a results-oriented objective, it should be possible to envision the result of achieving the objective.

Time-fixed. Objectives should indicate the time period during which we will achieve them, so as not to be open-ended. It is acceptable to include a range of completion dates to provide some degree of flexibility. Consider developing an implementation schedule for objectives and/or strategies, perhaps in 5-year increments.

Examples of Objectives Meeting the "SMART" Criteria

Biological Objectives:

Example 1.

To help restore the historic community structure of refuge grasslands, increase the cover of native plants from 50 to 80 percent, and native plant species richness from 30 to 50 species in mixed-grass habitats over the next 10 years.

Example 2.

Within 2 years of the plan's approval, conduct a baseline inventory to determine the existing composition and relative abundance of plant species in tallgrass prairie habitats on the refuge.

Visitor Services Objectives:

Example 1.

To develop support for refuge land acquisition, within 5 years of the plan's approval, 65 percent of the adult residents of Jefferson County will be aware of the economic contribution of the refuge to their community.

Example 2.

To guide long-term direction of the refuge's visitor services program, develop a demographic profile of refuge visitors within 2 years of the plan's approval.

Scientific Credibility

In addition to meeting the SMART criteria, base objectives on sound, documented, scientific information that affirms the management direction suggested by these criteria. Defensible objectives are based on the best information available and do not violate known scientific principles. Make every effort to locate, consult, and interpret documented data prior to developing objectives. Federal, State, and local agencies may be the source of additional information useful in developing sound, credible objectives. If available information is limited, base your decisions primarily on professional opinions or observations. In such instances, you might write objectives to direct the acquisition of needed data. Through the process of adaptive management, incorporate new information as it becomes available. Only where existing information is genuinely limited should you base your decisions on professional opinions and observations alone, and not just to save time and effort. Sound professional judgement should always be complemented by scientific corroboration when available.

Documenting the Rationale for Objectives

Document the rationale behind each objective. The rationale describes background/ history, assumptions, and technical details so that the reader can understand how the objective was formulated. The degree of documentation will vary, but at a minimum should include logic, assumptions, and sources of information such as scientific literature, refuge-specific data, and expert opinion. This promotes informed debate on the objective's merits, continuity in management through staff turnover, and reevaluation of the objective as new information becomes available.

Specifically, provide supporting data for the objective, note the source (e.g., peer-reviewed literature, unpublished data, observation, etc.), and describe how we applied the data. Cite authorities immediately following relevant statements (e.g., John Smith, pers. comm.; Doe, J. 1999) to indicate which sources apply to which statements and/or objectives. Include full citations at the end of the document. Additionally, define key terms to avoid misinterpretation and miscommunication, and assure measurability. For example, if you reference a "high-quality hunting experience," you must specify the criteria of a "high quality" hunt. If appropriate, document the sources of definitions to demonstrate they are not arbitrary.

The following example provides supporting rationale for a biological objective.

Grassland Objective

Over the next 15 years, convert 600 hectares of planted cover (dense nesting cover, introduced grasses, and warm season native grass plantings) to a diverse native floral community composed of 75 percent of the climax species identified in Heidel's Classification (1986).

Supporting Rationale:

The refuge has approximately 739 hectares of planted warm season native grass fields composed of three to four species including big bluestem, little bluestem, Indian grass, and switchgrass. Refuge nest records for the past 9 years indicate that these stands do not attract nesting waterfowl because they are lacking vegetative structural diversity. The refuge also has over 1,199 hectares of introduced grasses consisting primarily of smooth brome and Kentucky bluegrass. These fields were generally planted to some other cover type, but have been invaded. If these fields are managed with fire and haying, they do provide marginal nesting cover for species like blue-winged teal, but do not offer the structure preferred by many of the other nesting birds like bobolinks, mallards, and gadwalls (Smith and Brown 1993). A total of 600 hectares of planted cover would be converted to a diverse native floral community which involves intensive management. This total includes sites in the six prairie focus areas.

Section V

Concerns Specific to the Biological Program

Since the National Wildlife Refuge System Improvement Act of 1997 (Improvement Act) mandates that wildlife and wildlife conservation are a refuge's top priority, the biological program is the foundation of refuge management. We must carefully develop biological goals and objectives as the resource management effort depends on their appropriateness and achievability. Their development requires a thoughtful process of blending the refuge purpose(s), other legal directives, policy, goals of larger-scale plans, biological information, capabilities and limiting factors, and public input. Goals and objectives developed for other refuge programs will often complement those for the biological program and should never conflict with them.

Availability of Refuge Baseline Data

The availability of biotic and abiotic baseline data for individual refuges varies widely within the Refuge System. We generally lack comprehensive species inventories, including threatened and endangered species. This adds much uncertainty to the development and evaluation of objectives and strategies. If you have limited on-site baseline data, then rely on available scientific literature, refuge data files, State data, and/or expert opinion. In addition to typical resource objectives, develop a complement of objectives to identify and gather additional needed information.

Physical Limits to Achievability

Many refuges, particularly in the contiguous United States, are located in highly altered systems. Hydrology and topography have often been irreversibly changed, exotic species have become naturalized, some native species have disappeared, and a variety of artificial structures fill the landscape. In many cases, historic ecosystem function is not recoverable. You must develop goals and objectives that you can achieve within such constraints. For example, it may be unreasonable to propose restoration of highly altered topography or extirpation of naturalized species. The land must have the potential to produce the desired result and subsequently sustain desired conditions.

Base objectives on realistic assumptions. However, some problems that appear insurmountable might be addressed if we divide them into component parts or root causes, each with a separate objective. Flexibility in implementing strategies might also overcome apparent limitations. In Table 3, for example, the strategy used to meet Objective 1 under Example 2 may be understory thinning. However, this may only be possible when the Bureau of Reclamation, or perhaps natural drying, lowers the adjacent river sufficiently to allow access. While the timing and frequency of thinning may be outside your control, you could still write the objective. Supporting rationale for the objective would explain the situation.

Other Considerations

Table 3 illustrates the relationship between biological goals, objectives, and strategies. The palustrine wetlands goal in Example 1 references both a habitat type *and* two species groups of interest, thus providing some focus to the goal. In Example 2, we write the second objective to direct the collection of currently unavailable information. Example 3 demonstrates that you may employ visitor services strategies to achieve biological goals and objectives (and vice versa). Here the objective calls for reducing suspended sediment in runoff to reduce turbidity and raise water quality in streams. Community outreach to inform local farmers about the impacts of their land use practices can complement biological strategies, such as planting vegetative filter strips.

Table 3. Examples of Biological Goals, Objectives, and Strategies.

Goals	*Objectives*	*Strategies*
(G1) Palustrine Wetland: Maintain existing species diversity of migratory birds and resident amphibians in managed wetlands of the Mesa and Plains Physiographic Area.	(G1-1) Manage all palustrine wetlands in Unit A for dense (>75 percent of the water surface) annual vegetation flooded to a depth of less than 30 cm to maximize seed production for foraging fall (September-October) migrating dabbling ducks (e.g., teal, pintail, mallard).	Control water levels; conduct prescribed burns; disk or plow.
	(G1-2) Manage 500 ha of palustrine wetlands in Unit B for sparse (<25 percent of the water surface) annual or perennial vegetation flooded seasonally (March-July) to a depth of less than 5 cm for foraging dowitchers, avocets and teal, and nesting avocets.	Control water levels; conduct prescribed burns; disk or plow; graze livestock.
	(G1-3) Manage all palustrine wetlands in Unit C for dense (>75 percent of the water surface) perennial emergent vegetation, flooded seasonally (March-July) or semi-permanently to a depth of 10-45 cm for pairing, nesting, and foraging teal, foraging avocets and dowitchers, and breeding chorus frogs.	Control water levels.
(G2) Floodplain Forest: Provide conditions necessary to maximize breeding populations of Neotropical migratory birds, forest-nesting waterfowl, and Indiana bats in floodplain forests of the Prairie Peninsula Physiographic Area.	(G2-1) Provide large blocks (> x ha) of mature forest (trees > x in. dbh) with scattered large cottonwoods (xx percent canopy cover) and sparse understory (xx percent canopy cover) within 1/2 km of water for nesting and foraging wood ducks and nesting warblers.	Mechanically thin understory; conduct prescribed burns.
	(G2-2) Within 3 years of the plan's approval, conduct surveys in floodplain forests on the refuge from March to September to locate Indiana bat roost sites and to document habitat conditions (tree species and size, understory density, distance to water) used by this species.	Capture bats with mist nets; measure vegetation using nested quadrats.
(G3) Watershed: Restore the integrity and environmental health of the Sand Creek watershed to improve water quality for both wildlife and humans.	(G3-1) Within 3 years of the plan's approval, the suspended sediment concentration during peak flows in Sand Creek will not exceed the State standard of xx ppm.	Personally contact 25 percent of the active farmers within the watershed each year.
	(G3-2) Within 3 years of the plan's approval, the depth of annual silt deposition in the refuge's Sand Lake will be less than 3 cm per year.	With representatives from the Department of Agriculture and the State, sponsor a workshop on the use of filter strips.

Goals and Objectives for Unmanipulated Habitats

Since we often write biological goals in support of specific wildlife, habitat types, or ecological communities, a refuge with a greater complexity of resources might logically have more biological goals, and thus objectives, than one that is less complex. On the other hand, even on complex refuges we do not actively manipulate many habitats, communities, and wildlife taxa. In this case, you might develop goals and objectives to direct inventory, monitoring, and/or research, if appropriate. On the other hand, if no effort is to be directed at them, goals and or objectives for such resources would be unnecessary. Perhaps a single goal might address all unmanipulated resources. Use sound professional judgment in deciding and reference your decision in your document.

Illustrating the Flow from Goal to Objective to Strategy

Assume our goal is *"To restore historic levels of species diversity of declining grassland-dependent migratory birds and other indigenous wildlife in native tallgrass prairie habitat."* This provides a target (historic levels of species diversity) for a specific habitat (tallgrass prairie). It does not describe measurable features of the land that must exist to meet the target. These appear in the supporting objectives.

Through critical thinking, review of refuge files and scientific literature, and discussions with experts, key factors emerge. To restore diversity, we determine that tallgrass prairies must be very large, structurally diverse, and have a complex vegetation component. We then develop SMART objectives that describe the details of each required criteria. For example, part of an objective might require tallgrass patches in excess of 40 hectares to meet habitat requirements of specific target bird species. Additional details describe the desired floristic complexity by requiring, for example, that we increase native plant richness within patches from 20 species to 40 species.

Strategies are the specific actions, tools, or techniques used to meet objectives. We move from objective to strategy by selecting practices that applied on the ground, will achieve the SMART criteria of the objective. For example, assume an area contains two 16-hectare patches of tallgrass prairie separated by a 16-hectare cropfield. Converting the cropfield to prairie would create a contiguous block of 48 hectares, thus meeting the objective's size criteria. To improve floristic complexity, we might apply several strategies including burning, seeding, or grazing by native herbivores.

Following application of the selected strategies, we then monitor the habitat to determine if we achieved the objective. We use adaptive management to make any necessary modifications based on the results of the monitoring effort.

Section VI

Concerns Specific to the Visitor Services Program

The Improvement Act (Sec. 5(a)) states, *". . .compatible wildlife-dependent recreation . . . generally fosters refuge management and. . .can develop an appreciation for fish and wildlife."* This is reiterated in one of the national goals of the Refuge System (601 FW 1.8D), *"Provide and enhance opportunities to participate in compatible wildlife-dependent recreation, including hunting, fishing, wildlife observation and photography, and environmental education and interpretation."* Thus, while there is value in recreation for its own sake, and at times it may be appropriate to write goals emphasizing simple enjoyment of the refuge, ideally the outcome we seek through visitor services is appreciation of and support for fish and wildlife conservation.

We use the link between a wildlife-dependent use and public appreciation and support for wildlife as the basis for developing visitor services goals and objectives, though it may not always be readily apparent. The link is clear in an environmental education activity where school groups collect native seeds for habitat restoration. It may be less obvious, however, where a refuge visitor simply views an interpretive display, and even less so in the case of recreational fishing. Still, the link is there. All these activities promote a connection between people and wildlife. The premise of the Improvement Act and the Refuge System goal above is that, if people understand and appreciate wildlife, they will support the refuge as well as broader environmental issues. Support can be direct, such as becoming a refuge volunteer, or indirect, such as writing letters to the media and informed voting on environmental issues. Such evidence of support can be the measurable component in the "experience-based" approach to developing visitor services objectives described below.

The biggest challenge in writing objectives for a refuge's visitor services program is to think in terms of outcomes. Describe what you want to accomplish, not how you will accomplish it. The outcomes may suggest a clear link to our mission and the biological goals of a refuge. Or, you may state them such that the link to our mission is less obvious and involves several assumptions. The following discussion elaborates on this point.

Two Possible Approaches

There are two possible approaches to thinking about objectives for wildlife-dependent recreation:

(1) Opportunity-based approach
(2) Experience-based approach

It is possible to mix these approaches depending upon the topic and objective within any given plan.

Opportunity-based Approach. In this approach, the outcomes of the objective are visitor opportunities. We provide visitors specific opportunities to experience wildlife, measure and track what we provide, and assume that their appreciation for fish and wildlife increases. In this approach, our measurable outcomes might include kilometers of tour route, number of interpretive programs offered, observation decks provided, or days open to hunting. The outcomes are easy to measure, and they assume the appreciation we ultimately want to achieve.

Experience-based Approach. In this approach, outcomes of the objective are the specific changes in attitude, behavior, or knowledge we want visitors to experience. The recreational opportunities we provide are only tools to effect that change. An objective's desired outcome is the specific change we want to occur, and to what

degree. We monitor our success using visitor surveys or other instruments. In this approach, measurable outcomes might include percent of visitors reporting a high-quality hunting experience, number of local residents saying they strongly support the refuge, or percent of students who successfully complete an environmental education unit. While these outcomes are more difficult to measure, the link between activities we offer and the appreciation we ultimately want to achieve is tangible, demonstrated by a change in attitude, behavior, or knowledge.

Monitoring here is demanding. It may require a survey of the target audience, which involves time, effort, expense, and possibly approval of the Office of Management and Budget (OMB).

While the experience-based approach is the more precise and desirable approach for visitor services objectives, it is sometimes impractical due to the resources required to conduct the associated monitoring and evaluation. Therefore, in many instances we use the opportunity-based approach. In these cases, however, the rationale for the opportunity-based objective should mention the ulterior benefits that might result. For example, the rationale for a new trail might answer the who, why, what, and where of the trail: *"This trail will be developed at site X on the refuge so that it is easily accessible to the residents of community Y. We assume that hiking through the prairie will promote an appreciation for the biological diversity and wildlife value of a prairie, and ultimately promote support among the community for refuge efforts to restore and manage this habitat. A study of attitudinal changes of trail users in the Midwest (provide citation) justifies this assumption."* (The discussion in Section IV, Documenting The Rationale For Objectives, provides further guidance on elements of an effective rationale statement.)

To illustrate the two approaches, we can follow the evolution of a hypothetical refuge interpretive program. The refuge has no program and wants to begin one, and has developed the following goal: *"Residents of the local community understand and support the refuge's red wolf reintroduction program."* A simple interpretation objective might be to specify the number of interpretive programs (opportunities) we will offer each year. After a year or two, the staff reviews attendance records. If they decide the total people reached does not match the effort, they reformulate the interpretation objective in terms of people attending the programs (still an opportunity-based approach, but more difficult to achieve). They increase outreach to boost attendance. After 2 years, attendance records show they have met the objective. Still, the manager wonders, "Is our message getting through?" They again reformulate the objective to specify the percent of attendees who reflect attitudinal changes toward red wolf reintroduction (experience-based). Until now, monitoring was easy—track total programs offered and the number of people attending. Now, however, assessing success requires a survey of attendees, which might involve issues of survey design and administrative approvals.

The Context for Visitor Services Goals and Objectives

Articulating visitor services goals and objectives presents challenges not seen in the biological program. The Improvement Act requires that we facilitate the six priority public uses (hunting, fishing, wildlife observation and photography, environmental education and interpretation) where compatible. However, providing for the needs of wildlife is our top priority on refuges. Providing opportunities for compatible priority public uses is our second priority. Additionally, management of priority public uses must follow Service guidance for minimum standards in visitor services and customer service.

Within these considerations—and given the range of possible topics within visitor services—how do we choose focus areas for visitor services goals and objectives? Various possibilities arise. We could write individual goals for each priority use, as well as additional goals addressing outreach, general visitor services, and other topics. More practically, one might find creative ways to develop fewer but more focused goals that combine these various activities.

Another approach might be to focus on audiences. One goal might deal with refuge visitors. Another goal might deal with the public in the surrounding community. Or, a goal might deal with a particular subset of visitors—students, for example. Whichever approach and organization you choose, develop goals and objectives that promote support for the refuge and wildlife while reflecting refuge purpose(s), Refuge System mission and goals, and the significance and/or uniqueness of the refuge as reflected in its vision statement. Address national, regional, and ecosystem goals related to visitor services and uses, and incorporate State fish and wildlife conservation or outdoor recreation plans, community demographics, customer satisfaction studies, the origin of visitors, and other socioeconomic or demographic information, as appropriate.

Illustrating the Flow from Goal to Objective to Strategy

Suppose we want to develop recreational hunting with the assumption it will promote appreciation for wildlife among hunters who will then support the refuge. We also assume a quality hunt experience will enhance their appreciation. We state that "quality" pertains to specific criteria related to safety, ethics, impacts on wildlife, and similar elements. A goal could be, *"To provide a high-quality refuge waterfowl hunt that generates hunter support for the refuge's migratory bird management program."* An objective related to this goal might be, *"Host 1,000 to 1,600 high-quality waterfowl hunting visits annually."* To monitor our success, we state a rationale for the objective that quantifies our measurable criteria for "high quality."

For example, the *safety* standard means no hunting-related safety incidents, and the ethics standard requires that we cite less than 3 percent of hunters for hunting violations. The *opportunity* requires there be no unmet request for access by hunters with disabilities, and the *crowding* standard says that parties will be spaced at least 360 meters apart. We then select strategies, which might include developing a brochure that stresses safety and ethical behavior, pre-season orientation, law enforcement, and opportunities for disabled hunters.

On this basis, we could monitor several parameters to measure success without surveying the hunters. However, after a few years the refuge staff may want to know if they are providing the desired hunting experience from the hunters' perspective. In that case, we implement a survey to determine if hunters feel safe and uncrowded and if they recommend the hunt to others. You must design and implement the survey in accordance with existing laws, regulations, and policies, including OMB standards for compliance with the Paperwork Reduction Act. Table 4 presents additional examples of visitor services goals, objectives, and strategies.

Table 4. Examples of Visitor Services Goals, Objectives, and Strategies.

Goals	_Objectives_	_Strategies_
(G1) Interpretation: Refuge visitors appreciate the refuge's importance to waterfowl and support the refuge's resource conservation efforts.	(G1-1) Within 5 years of the plan's approval, at least 75 percent of visitors will understand the refuge's contribution to reversing ongoing wetland losses throughout the United States. _(Experience-based)_	Develop interpretive exhibits in proximity to wetland restoration sites that focus on the importance of protecting wetland habitats. Create a wayside exhibit at the start of the auto tour route which depicts the plight of wetland habitats throughout the United States.
	(G1-2) Within 3 years of the plan's approval, more than 75 percent of refuge visitors will be able to identify migratory waterfowl management as a primary purpose of the refuge. _(Experience-based)_	In cooperation with the local Audubon Chapter, sponsor guided birdwatching opportunities during the waterfowl migration.
(G2) Outreach: Promote awareness within the Eastern Shore community of the unique value of the lower Delmarva Peninsula to Neotropical and temperate migratory birds.	(G2-1) Within 3 years of the plan's approval, more than 50 percent of adults residing within 40 kilometers of the visitor center will have visited the refuge. _(Opportunity-based)_	Install a local radio transmitter that interprets the waterfowl migration. Place an advertisement for the refuge in the local outdoor guide; host a media day each year; publish up to ten articles a year in the local community paper.
	(G2-2) Within 1 year of the plan's approval, all realtors and land developers in Northampton County will see or hear the message that it is important to preserve existing hardwoods as staging habitat for Neotropical migratory birds. _(Opportunity-based)_	Conduct two workshops for local realtors and developers to encourage them to educate clients on practices they can employ to enhance the habitat value of their property during and after home construction.
(G3) Customer Service: Visitors of all abilities will feel welcome and enjoy a safe visit to an area that they recognize as a national wildlife refuge.	(G3-1) In a biannual random survey, at least 90 percent of visitors will report that they felt welcome and had an enjoyable visit, and they will be able to identify the area as a national wildlife refuge. _(Experience-based)_	Conduct a biannual visitor survey.
	(G3-2) Within 1 year of the CCP's approval, construct a wheelchair accessible observation point for wildlife viewing along the auto tour route. _(Opportunity-based)_	Request design assistance from disabled special interest groups.

Section VII

Other Refuge Programs

You will find many opportunities to apply the techniques in this handbook to other refuge programs. Experiment with the approach anywhere it can help you describe management direction for a particular program area. Tables 5 and 6 provide examples for wilderness and cultural resource applications.

Table 5. Examples of Goals, Objectives, and Strategies for Other Refuge Programs: Cultural Resources.

Goals	*Objectives*	*Strategies*
(G1) The cultural resources and cultural history of the refuge are valued and preserved, and connect refuge staff, visitors, and the community to the area's past.	(G1-1) Within 1 year of the plan's approval, prepare National Register of Historic Places determinations of eligibility or nomination forms for all qualified structures.	Consult with the State Historic Preservation Officer and the local historical society during the review to determine National Register eligibility.
	(G1-2) Within 2 years of the plan's approval, complete condition surveys for all eligible or nominated structures.	Contract with a qualified historic architectural organization to complete evaluations of refuge historic structures and condition surveys.
	(G1-3) Within 3 years of the plan's approval, develop a historic structure management plan for all National Register eligible or listed structures.	Contract with a qualified organization to complete a historic structure management plan. Include condition assessments for all National Register eligible structures; assess management alternatives and priorities; consult with the State Historic Preservation Officer on necessary steps to fulfill the refuge's responsibilities under the National Historic Preservation Act.
(G2) Identify and protect prehistoric archaeological resources on the refuge which are eligible for or listed in the National Register of Historic Places.	(G2-1) Within 1 year of the plan's approval, complete a thorough literature review of the refuge's cultural resources.	Contract with a qualified organization to complete a cultural resource literature review.
	(G2-2) Within 3 years of the plan's approval, undertake appropriate surveys to identify important archaeological resources within the refuge.	Contract with a qualified organization to complete archaeological surveys.
	(G2-3) Within 5 years of the plan's completion, stabilize or recover significant eroding archaeological resources within the refuge.	Consult with the State Historic Preservation Officer and regional archaeologist regarding appropriate stabilization techniques.

Table 6. Examples of Goals, Objectives, and Strategies for Other Refuge Programs: Wilderness[1].

Goals	_Objectives_	_Strategies_
(G1) Protect and restore the biological integrity, diversity, and environmental health of the low sagebrush community of the Columbia Plateau to help preserve its wilderness character.	(G1-1) To decrease the imprint of human activity, within 5 years of the plan's approval, remove artificial structures apparent to visitors at trailheads A, B, and C, and camping areas D, and E that are not necessary to administer the wilderness.	Burn and/or recycle wooden structures; use volunteers to dismantle and haul out remaining materials by hand.
	(G1-2) In the 10 years following the plan's approval, prevent the infestation of cheat grass and Canada thistle into all unaffected areas to maintain native plant diversity and naturalness.	Employ integrated pest management techniques; use prescribed fire; develop and implement regulations to control weed entry (control diet of pack stock, hikers must clean boots prior to entry, etc.).
	(G1-3) Within 1 year of the plan's approval, determine high-priority areas for invasive plant removal based on level of threat, potential for reinfestation, etc., targeting areas where treatment will be most effective.	Conduct literature search; conduct research; engage in expert consultation.
	(G1-4) Over years 2-6 following the plan's approval, reduce by 50 percent the high-priority acreage infested with cheat grass and Canada thistle to increase reestablishment of native vegetation.	Employ integrated pest management techniques; use prescribed fire; develop and implement regulations to control weed entry (control diet of pack stock, hikers must clean boots prior to entry, etc.).
	(G1-5) Within 2 years of the plan's approval, eliminate 50 percent of the illegal outdoor recreation vehicle use.	Conduct education and outreach; block trailheads; add law enforcement patrols.
(G2) Promote an understanding of wilderness values and _Leave No Trace_ principles among visitors to preserve the opportunity for outstanding wilderness experiences.	(G2-1) Within 1 year of the plan's approval, all refuge personnel will incorporate _Leave No Trace_ principles into their work to help retain the wilderness character.	Conduct education and outreach (distribute brochures, show _Leave No Trace_ video, develop TV ads, erect displays, etc.); establish partnerships.
	(G2-2) Within 2 years of the plan's approval, 50 percent of wilderness visitors will support and value the refuge wilderness, resulting in responsible recreation behavior.	Engage in education and outreach (show _Wild By Law_ video, develop TV ads, erect displays, develop brochure, etc.); establish partnerships.
	(G2-3) Within 5 years of the plan's approval, 75 percent of visitors will be using _Leave No Trace_ principles to preserve wild conditions for future users.	Offer training; sponsor _Leave No Trace_ workshop; offer awards and other incentives.

[1] Assume that we have subjected each of the wilderness objectives and strategies shown here to a minimum requirement analysis and that they reflect the minimum tool necessary for management of the area.

References

National Wildlife Refuge System Administration Act of 1966, as amended by the
National Wildlife Refuge System Improvement Act of 1997, 16 U.S.C. 668dd-668ee.

601 FW 1, National Wildlife Refuge System Mission and Goals, and Refuge Purposes.

602 FW 1, Refuge Planning Overview.

602 FW 3, Comprehensive Conservation Planning Process.

602 FW 4, Step-Down Management Planning.

Acknowledgments

The need for guidance on goals and objectives for refuge management arose out of
grassland workshops held in the Mountain - Prairie Region (Region 6) of the U.S. Fish
and Wildlife Service in the early 1990s. An informal handbook with limited circulation
was drafted in 1996.

However, with the rise of Comprehensive Conservation Planning pursuant to the
National Wildlife Refuge System Improvement Act of 1997, the need for more formal
and detailed guidance became apparent. The present handbook is in response to this
need.

The authors acknowledge those who drafted the original guidance, as well as the
individuals and groups who reviewed and contributed to the present handbook. Among
those are the Regional Refuge Biologists, Planning Chiefs, and Visitor Services Chiefs.
Thanks to all.

Appendix A.

Examples of Biological Objectives and How Well They Meet the "SMART" Criteria

These examples illustrate the application of the SMART criteria. An acceptable objective meets all five of the criteria. You must derive objectives through a logical, reasoned approach, using existing information. A combination of critical thinking and adhering to the SMART criteria will yield the best objectives.

Example 1.

Habitat Objective

Restore and maintain native grassland and riparian communities within the refuge to meet the needs of native flora and fauna.

Evaluation of this Objective Using the SMART Criteria

Specific:

This objective does not provide enough detail to understand what specific structure or composition or other habitat features are necessary to provide for the needs of the native flora and fauna. The words "restore" and "maintain," in and of themselves, provide inadequate detail.

Measurable:

This objective is not measurable, and we cannot determine progress toward its achievement. There is no clear description of the structure or composition or other habitat features that would indicate, in a measurable way, when we have effectively restored or maintained the habitat.

Achievable:

Because the objective is not specific or measurable, our ability to achieve it is impossible to discern.

Results-oriented:

The objective does not describe exactly what will result from its achievement.

Time-fixed:

There is no defined time period for the achievement of the objective.

How Well the Objective Meets the SMART Criteria:

This objective does not meet the SMART criteria. To remedy the situation, the objective must specify the structure, composition, or other habitat features that describe the desired condition and indicate, in a measurable way, when we have achieved this condition. It also must denote a specific end point and the time period for accomplishing the objective.

Objective Rewritten to Meet the SMART Criteria:

We would improve the objective by calling for the following in grassland habitat:

Provide native grassland patches that exceed 40 contiguous hectares in size, have an average late May-early June VOR (visual obstruction rating) of >20 centimeters, and >10 species of native forbs per 0.4 hectare to provide breeding habitat for grassland birds of management concern.

Example 2.

Riparian Habitat Objective

Treat, restore, and protect a minimum of 50 hectares of riparian habitat per year for the benefit of migratory birds.

Evaluation of this Objective Using the SMART Criteria

Specific:

Note that the objective applies to riparian habitat. The phrase "a minimum of 50 hectares" makes it clear how much habitat we are considering within the objective. However, this objective does not provide enough detail to understand what specific structure or composition or other habitat features are needed to benefit migratory birds. The words "treat," "restore," and "protect" provide inadequate detail.

Measurable:

The only part of this objective that is measurable is "a minimum of 50 hectares." There is no clear description of the structure or composition or other habitat features that would indicate, in a measurable way, when we have appropriately treated, restored, or protected the habitat.

Achievable:

Because the objective has aspects that are not specific or measurable, our ability to achieve it is impossible to discern.

Results-oriented:

The objective does not describe exactly what will result from its achievement.

Time-fixed:

The objective does call for a time period ("per year") within which we are to accomplish it.

How Well the Objective Meets the SMART Criteria:

This objective does not meet all of the SMART criteria. To provide a meaningful and measurable target for management, the objective needs to clearly specify the desired structure and composition of the riparian habitat. It also must indicate a specific management direction.

Objective Rewritten to Meet the SMART Criteria:

Restore 50 hectares per year of dense (60-100 percent canopy closure) willow in patches >0.5 hectare and >10 meters wide to connect existing willow patches to provide nesting habitat for Neotropical migratory birds.

Example 3.

<u>Dry Forest Stand Structure Objective</u>

Over the long term (100-200 years), aim for a mosaic of dry forest stands of different age and structural classes at approximately the same seral distributions as occurred historically (~15% early seral, ~35% mid seral, and ~50% old single or old multi-layer [Quigley and Arbelbide 1997]).

Evaluation of this Objective Using the SMART Criteria

Specific:

The habitat type (dry forest) is specified. The objective calls for a mosaic of seral stages and denotes specific percentages of each stage that we desire. We could improve the objective by describing the block sizes or desired spatial distribution of the various seral stages. We need to include definitions of early, mid, and old seral stages and any specific structural or compositional characteristics in the supporting rationale for the objective. Referring only to the citation, without the accompanying details, provides inadequate specificity. The objective requires only that the refuge "aim for" the desired conditions. A more specific phrase would be to require the refuge to "achieve" the desired conditions.

Measurable:

This objective is only measurable as stated if we clearly define and enumerate the desired structure and composition of each seral stage in the accompanying text. If we do not provide such details, the objective is not measurable.

Achievable:

As noted under the "Specific" criteria, we should change the wording of the objective from "aim for" to "achieve."

Results-oriented:

The objective is results-oriented and provides a general description of the desired results. We could improve it with the addition of details as described under the "Specific" criteria.

Time-fixed:

The objective provides a long-term time frame within which we are to achieve it. However, it would be useful to develop some intermediate milestones (e.g., every 5 or 10 years) to help gauge progress toward meeting the objective. Such checkpoints would help determine if the habitat is progressing in the proper direction and allows for adaptive management and minor adjustments along the way.

How Well the Objective Meets the SMART Criteria:

This objective meets the SMART criteria, but we could improve it with a few additional details as noted above.

Objective Rewritten to Meet the SMART Criteria:

Over the long term (100-200 years), achieve a mosaic of dry forest stands of different age and structural classes at approximately the same seral distributions as occurred historically: ~15% early seral, ~35% mid seral, and ~50% old single or old multi-layer (Quigley and Arbelbide 1997). Within 15 years, ensure that ~15% is in an early seral stage, and other areas are succeeding toward mid and old stages based on increases in diameter and canopy cover.

Example 4.

Tundra Habitat Objective

Obtain baseline data on vegetation composition (plant species abundance, frequency, and dominance) and structure (canopy cover and height) of tundra habitat within 2 years of the plan's approval.

Evaluation of this Objective Using the SMART Criteria

Specific:

The objective specifies the habitat type and describes the type of baseline data to be collected.

Measurable:

Although it can be determined whether or not baseline data were collected, it is not clear from the objective how many data points or plots are required. The objective could be improved by noting that a specified number of plots or transects will be established per unit area, or the data will meet specified statistical standards.

Achievable:

The objective is achievable.

Results-oriented:

The objective will accomplish a specific result upon its completion.

Time-fixed:

The objective notes the time period within which it is to be accomplished.

How Well the Objective Meets the SMART Criteria:

This objective meets the SMART criteria, with the exception of the additional details noted under the "Measurable" criteria.

Objective Rewritten to Meet the SMART Criteria:

Obtain baseline data on vegetation composition (plant species abundance, frequency, and dominance) and structure (canopy cover and height) of tundra habitat within 2 years of the CCP's approval. Data will meet the minimum statistical standard of being within 20 percent of the mean at the 80 percent confidence level."

Note: This objective applies to pristine or wilderness habitats where natural processes are in place and no active habitat management is intended. The intent of the objective is to gather baseline data on the plant communities of the refuge, which we could then follow by habitat monitoring to detect changes, such as invasion by exotics or significant changes in vegetative structure and/or composition.

Example 5.

<u>Upland Forest Habitat Objective</u>

Maintain 100 hectares of upland forest habitat as a buffer between neighboring agricultural lands and refuge wetlands, and survey the 100-hectare upland forest every 3 years to determine the presence and abundance of any exotic or invasive vegetation.

Evaluation of this Objective Using the SMART Criteria

Specific:

In general, the objective is clearly worded and specific. Additional details describing which plants we consider exotic or invasive would be useful.

Measurable:

The objective calls for maintaining the 100 hectares in upland forest, which we can measure and track. Presence and abundance of exotic or invasive plants are measurable items.

Achievable:

The objective is achievable.

Results-oriented:

The objective will accomplish a specific result upon its completion.

Time-fixed:

The objective notes the time period over which we are to accomplish it.

How Well the Objective Meets the SMART Criteria:

This objective meets the SMART criteria, assuming that we define exotic or invasive vegetation elsewhere in the text.

Objective Rewritten to Meet the SMART Criteria:

Maintain 100 hectares of upland forest as a buffer between neighboring agricultural lands and refuge wetlands, and survey the 100-hectare upland forest every 3 years to determine the presence and abundance of any exotic or invasive vegetation (of present concern are garlic mustard, glossy buckthorn, and Japanese honeysuckle; to be updated as new information becomes available).

Note: This objective applies to areas on a refuge that we manage in a largely custodial manner. For example, the primary focus of a refuge may be on managing wetlands, yet it also may contain 100 hectares of upland forest that we would like to keep in forest but not manipulate extensively as we would wetlands.

Appendix B.

Examples of Visitor Services Objectives and How Well They Meet the "SMART" Criteria

These examples illustrate the application of the SMART criteria to public use objectives. Adhering to the SMART criteria will yield acceptable objectives. An advantage of using the SMART criteria is that the criteria encourage critical thinking in addressing issues and identifying gaps in knowledge and understanding.

Example 1.

Environmental Education Objective

Encourage schools to use the refuge to teach students about the natural world. Develop a cadre of teachers who use the refuge for environmental education within the next 5 years and thereafter, and recruit at least one new teacher per year. Within 10 years of the plan's approval, the refuge will receive five teacher-led class visits each year.

Evaluation of this Objective Using the SMART Criteria

Specific:

This objective is far too general. It contains three components. The first two—"Encourage schools. . ." and "Develop a cadre. . ." —tend to be input or action oriented. These can be seen as a means for achieving the third component, "Within 10 years of. . ." The last sentence has several of the characteristics of a good objective. The objective could be made more specific by limiting it to only the last sentence.

Measurable:

If we limit the objective to the last sentence, it is measurable.

Achievable:

Without knowing more details, we can assume that the objective is achievable.

Results-oriented:

Only the last sentence of the objective is results-oriented. The other parts of the objective suggest strategies we will use to accomplish the desired result.

Time-fixed:

A time period is defined in the last sentence.

How Well the Objective Meets the SMART Criteria:

This objective has some of the characteristics of a good objective. By editing the objective statement to the last sentence, we improve it. If the refuge's education program is a long-standing one, one criticism would be that we should focus the objective more on outcomes. In such cases, we might recast the objective to state what the students from the five classroom visits will know after visiting the refuge.

Objective Rewritten to Meet the SMART Criteria:

Within 10 years of the plan's approval, the refuge will receive five teacher-led class visits each year.

Example 2.

<u>Interpretation Objective</u>

Promote public awareness and advocacy of refuge resources and management activities that conserve the region's natural, cultural, and historic resources in the visitor center and use signs, exhibits, pamphlets, and programs elsewhere on the refuge complex.

Evaluation of this Objective Using the SMART Criteria

Specific:

This objective statement is general and input-oriented rather than specific and outcome oriented. "Awareness and advocacy" and "public" are open to broad interpretation.

Measurable:

This objective is not measurable.

Achievable:

Because the objective is not specific or measurable, it is not possible to determine if it is achievable.

Results-oriented:

This objective is action-oriented. "Promote" and "use" are action words, not outcome words. The focus of the desired result is "awareness and advocacy," which we should describe in a way that permits its measurement.

Time-fixed:

This objective is not time-fixed.

How Well the Objective Meets the SMART Criteria:

This objective does not meet the SMART criteria. We need to recast the objective. Begin by thinking in terms of outcomes. We need to further specify the audience, outcomes and their measurements, and a realistic time frame for accomplishing the objective. In addition, the objective should avoid suggesting strategies (". . . use signs, exhibits, pamphlets, and programs. . .") to accomplish the objective.

Objective Rewritten to Meet the SMART Criteria:

Over the life of the plan, as measured in annual increments, the awareness and support of the refuge among visitors will have a positive trend as measured by visitor response cards distributed at the visitor center and trailheads.

Example 3.

<u>Fishing Objective</u>

Provide high-quality stream fishing opportunities to approximately 2,000 visitors per year, providing participants with reasonable harvest opportunities, uncrowded conditions, minimal conflicts with other users, and an opportunity to use various angling techniques.

Evaluation of this Objective Using the SMART Criteria

<u>Specific:</u>

This objective does a good job in conveying what we will provide. A subsequent discussion might further define in quantifiable terms what we mean by "reasonable harvest opportunities, uncrowded conditions, . . ."

<u>Measurable:</u>

If we put "harvest opportunities, uncrowded conditions, minimal conflicts with other users, and an opportunity to use various angling techniques" in quantifiable terms, the objective would be measurable.

<u>Achievable:</u>

Assuming that we met the above conditions of measurability, and we knew more about the refuge, we would be able to evaluate whether or not the objective is achievable.

<u>Results-oriented:</u>

This objective is results-oriented. "High-quality stream fishing opportunities for approximately 2,000 visitors per year" describes the target.

<u>Time-fixed:</u>

There is no defined time period for achieving the objective. We could improve the objective by beginning the statement with a phrase such as "By 2005," or "Within 4 years of adopting the plan. . ."

<u>How Well the Objective Meets the SMART Criteria:</u>

This objective has the potential to meet the SMART criteria with a small amount of editing and complementary discussion.

<u>Objective Rewritten to Meet the SMART Criteria:</u>

Within 4 years of the plan's approval, provide high-quality fishing opportunities to approximately 2,000 visitors per year, providing participants with reasonable harvest opportunities, uncrowded conditions, minimal conflicts with other users, and an opportunity to use various angling techniques.

Example 4.

<u>Wildife-dependent Recreation Objective</u>

Provide opportunities for wildlife photography, wildlife observation, hunting, and fishing.

Evaluation of this Objective Using the SMART Criteria

<u>Specific:</u>

This objective is not specific.

<u>Measurable:</u>

This objective is not measurable.

<u>Achievable:</u>

Because the objective is not specific or measurable, it is not possible to evaluate whether it is achievable or not.

<u>Results-oriented:</u>

Although the objective suggests that "opportunities" are the result we desire, the lack of specificity makes it impossible to know what is intended.

<u>Time-fixed:</u>

The objective is not time-fixed.

<u>How Well the Objective Meets the SMART Criteria:</u>

This opportunity-based objective does not meet the SMART criteria. The statement is closer to a goal statement than an objective statement. It may be appropriate to divide it into three objectives—one to cover photography and observation, one for hunting, and another for fishing.

<u>Objective Rewritten to Meet the SMART Criteria:</u>

Within 2 years of adoption of the CCP, two accessible observation blinds with a capacity for four people as indicated on the facilities map will be available to the public.

Example 5.

Environmental Education and
Interpretation Objective

*Make visitor contacts more effective to
increase visitors' awareness of the refuge,
its programs, and the National Wildlife
Refuge System. Visitors will know that the
trails go through diverse habitats, have a
general type of wildlife on the refuge, and
recognize the importance of undisturbed
areas and management activities on the
refuge.*

Evaluation of this Objective Using the SMART Criteria

Specific:

Although general, this objective's strength is that it begins to get at the types of
outcomes that we desire among visitors. We could improve the statement and make it
more specific by deleting the first sentence, which is action-oriented, and further
defining the specific content of what it is we want the visitor to know. For example, we
could expand a portion of the second sentence to read, "By 2004, 90 percent of adult
visitors who have been on the interpretive trail, will correctly match habitat labels to
pictures with a score of 80 percent."

Measurable:

The objective is not measurable in its present form, but could be made measurable by
incorporating the above suggestions.

Achievable:

With increased specificity and measurability, we could evaluate whether this objective is
measurable or not.

Results-oriented:

With the exception of the first sentence, the objective is results-oriented. We could
rewrite the first sentence to emphasize the desired result—"Visitors will be aware of
the refuge, its programs, and the National Wildlife Refuge System." To meet the other
criteria of a good objective, this sentence should include a desired level of awareness
and a time component.

Time-fixed:

There is no defined time period for this objective.

How Well the Objective Meets the SMART Criteria:

This statement has the potential to be a strong objective with some editing and
additions. As it now stands, the statement does not meet the SMART criteria.

Objective Rewritten to Meet the SMART Criteria:

*Within 4 years of the plan's approval, 80 percent of adult visitors will recognize:
(1) that refuge trails go through diverse habitats; (2) the type of wildlife on the refuge;
(3) the importance of undisturbed areas; and (4) refuge management activities when
presented with multiple choices in a nonrandom survey.*